Solid Small Business Marketing Advice for You… The Boss

Mike Dolpies

Printed in the U.S.A.

Published By: Ocean View Publishing, LLC

Marketing Consigliere
Solid Small Business Marketing Advice for You... The Boss

ISBN: 1532715552
ISBN-13: 978-1532715556

Preface

What is a "Consigliere?"

Consigliere (Italian consigliere "counselor", pronounced kohn-seel-yehr-eh) is a position within the leadership structure of Sicilian, Calabrian and American Mafia. The word was popularized by the novel The Godfather (1969), and its film adaptation. In the novel, a consigliere is an adviser or counselor to the boss, with the additional responsibility of representing the boss in important meetings both within the boss's crime family and with other crime families. The consigliere is a close, trusted friend and confidant, the mob's version of an elder statesman. In some depictions, he is devoid of ambition and dispenses disinterested advice. This passive image of the consigliere does not correspond with what little is known of real-life consiglieri, however. By the very nature of the job, a consigliere is one of the few in the family who can argue with the boss, and is often tasked with challenging the boss when needed to ensure subsequent plans are foolproof.

A real-life Mafia consigliere is generally the number three person in a crime family, after the boss and underboss in most cases. The boss, underboss, and consigliere constitute a three-man ruling panel, or "Administration."

I want you to know...this is not an invitation to join the Mob. This book is about giving you what you want and what you need when it comes to your marketing.

Perspective, guidance and solid advice for you, The Boss!

Table of Contents

Chapter 1: Just Say NO to Shiny New Objects 1

Chapter 2: Don't Let Your House Fall Apart 5

Chapter 3: Being Found and Capitalizing on "Intent Marketing" 9

Chapter 4: The Simple Secrets to an Awesome Online Reputation Marketing 11

Chapter 5: The "Push-Button" Secret Hiding in Plain Sight 21

Chapter 6: Are You Nuts Not to Have One of These? 27

Chapter 7: KEEP It Fresh 43

Chapter 8: The Linchpin of Social Media Marketing (And Maybe ALL Marketing) 45

Chapter 9: What to Say 49

Chapter 10: The Smart Money Uses Landing Pages 53

Chapter 11: All This "Marketing Stuff" Doesn't Matter Much if You Can't Sell 55

Chapter 12: Never Be Done 59

Introduction

In this book we're going to outline a simple online/offline marketing game-plan for your business.

Think of each of these concepts as a separate category. Each category can then produce its own sub-categories. A sub-list if you will. It will be up to you to constantly evolve the sub-list.

This marketing game-plan applies to your business if...

1. You serve a market with a specifically targeted geographic footprint.
2. You go on-site to perform work for clients and customers.
3. Customers/clients come to your place of business.

The Big Picture.

Don't read too much into all of the different categories and sub-categories of marketing. Fact is: For your business to grow you need to do as many things as possible to promote it within budget, time and reality. Most of the principles we discuss will be "Online Marketing" related. Why? Because marketing is about going where the eye-balls are. Most of the eyes are glued to screens... laptops, smartphones, etc.

Focus is key.

Having clear objectives is where online marketing success starts.

Quick Story... I know this might not relate to you – but stay with me. It's important...

I talked to an independent retail chain with a bunch of locations. Beyond having a less than spectacular website, virtually no online plan and an un-clear business identity on the web (we'll talk about that later) their main issue began at the core. It was simple... their website was built on a platform meant for online commerce. In discussions it was pretty clear... They had no desire to sell online. Their target customer is someone who enjoys shopping local. Basically... a total miss-match between what they wanted to happen as a result of their online marketing efforts and the web platform chosen.

This happens all the time. No clear objectives set prior to setting out online.

Since 2004...

Since 2004 I have been involved in online marketing. The funny part... My first website was one of those horrible and cheap things you get when someone "owes you a favor or money." It really did not work to do anything but take up space online. Then, in 2005, I met a woman that would become the future co-owner of one of my companies. She helped me build a website that had a clear objective... Getting folks to show up at my place of business.

Selling Online...

In 2006 I began selling online. What I did with my online business at the time was different than driving store traffic. I sold information: Tools, training, ideas and business advice to a specific vertical market. That's known as "niche information marketing." There are plenty of "Gurus" who will happily take your money and teach you "information marketing. To this day I still sell products on the web.

Fast Forward to 2010...

In 2010 we (my company) began helping a diverse set of businesses with online marketing. Our list of services consists of Website Design and Development, Search Engine Marketing, Facebook Ads management, Social Medial Consulting, Website Maintenance, Blogging and Mobile Apps. What our diverse clients have in common is they all serve a specific geographic market area.

The rest of this book will dive into a few details to keep you focused online. As a local business you have to be careful about how you spend your time. There are so many rabbit holes to fall down. I want to help you stay clear of the rabbit holes so you can focus and grow.

OK... Let's go...

Chapter 1:

Just Say NO to Shiny New Objects

You know Warren Buffet right? –He's one of the richest people in the world!

He's got a long-time biz partner.... Charlie Munger.

Obviously Buffet is careful about his business decisions.

Over the years... he has looked to Munger to advise him on things.

Munger earned the nickname... the "abominable no man."

That's because he often... tells Buffet "NO."

As in... "NO, this is not a good idea."

And when it comes to shiny new marketing objects you need to take a page from the "abominable no man."

You can't say "yes" to every new marketing thing that pops up.

But you do have to keep an eye on things.

The most important considerations...

One... Audience. And Two... are YOUR possible, customers, clients and members there?"
Example...

Twitter. I predicted Twitter's stock would tank. I was right. It's because their audience is weak. How can they command advertiser dollars... especially from us small biz owners? Exactly... NO!

Next... Live-stream social media apps.

These apps enable you to broadcast live to your followers. Periscope and Merrkat are the most popular.

But again... audience. Should you say "NO" to live streaming social media?" I don't know... are your prospects, customers and clients there watching live-streams on mobile?

BTW... Facebook launched live video and Merrkat got out of the business. You see how quickly things can change?
The fun and challenge with the shiny new object thing is you just never know. Before this book went to print Merrkat was no longer in the game.

You never know if the new thing is going to stick around.

In the 90's who knew websites would become a vital link in the marketing chain?

When email marketing first came on the scene – it was hard to tell how much it would impact marketing. Email returns $40 to every $1 spent.

When Google first started to over-take Yahoo... who knew that eventually it would power 65% of all searches... You HAVE TO be on Google.

And... Facebook... well... 1 Billion plus people a day scroll through their newsfeed and Facebook Ads are one of the most power marketing tools ever to come to us earthlings. Facebook was a shiny new object at one point.

Mobile Apps... I still run into those who think a mobile app is a "New Shiny Object." But then, you just look around at everyone staring down at their phones and realize you can engage them easily on that mobile channel.

Online Reviews... When online reviews first came on the scene – no one believed that they'd one day hold as much weight as the recommendation of a friend or family member. The critics thought Jeff Bezos, (Amazon Founder) was crazy for allowing reviews of books in the early days of Amazon.

Things that actually work eventually become dull. They are

no longer shiny and new. That's a good thing. Why? Because as the A-D-D crowd shifts to the shiny object you can be getting the old one to work for your business.

Chapter 2:

Don't Let Your House Fall Apart

Gone are the days of just slapping a website up and forgetting about it. Consumers are smart. They understand what they are looking for when it comes to finding the right information online. Consumers want information so they can make educated decisions and feel good about those decisions.

Your website must be maintained. It must always be an accurate and professional representation of your business. If your website is out of date – you have a problem. When I tell folks this they're often skeptical. Of course, I don't blame them. After all... I am the guy selling websites and online marketing.

Seriously... Websites that are outdated are a problem. Did you know Fox Small Business, Entrepreneur and many other small business news outlets have reported on studies that showed a high percentage of consumers would not trust a business with an outdated or unprofessional website. I guess the feeling... is, "Wow...If this business does not care about how their website looks – why would they care about me as a customer/client?"

We did a website redesign project for a company that once

lost a bid because of their tired old website. I found this out by asking the client prior to getting started... "So why are we redesigning this website?" He told me the story about how one prospect held several bids side by side. Still un-decided the prospect went and checked all of the websites for the companies that submitted bids. Needless to say – prior to the redesign – the website was pretty bad and these guys did not get the contract.

Guess what... This same scenario happened to us. We were in the process of redesigning our own website. Remember the "shoemaker's kids?" Their shoes are not the best because the shoemaker is busy making shoes for others – is that how the saying goes? Well... our site was falling behind. And we lost a bid because, all things being equal – the company we quoted did their final homework and checked our website. They did not like our website because it was out-dated. Of course, we finished our "redesign" and this has not been a problem since.

Your website is not static! Change offers and calls-to-action from time to time. Test new ideas. Watch your analytic reports and make educated decisions based on data. If something is not working – change it!

Code Maintenance is another reason to keep things updated. If your website is built on a CMS (Content Management System) you must keep it secure. Update the "plug-ins" and update the platform for the latest security protocol. It is no fun when a website gets hacked. Proper maintenance can prevent any issues.

Chapter 3:

Being Found and Capitalizing on "Intent Marketing"

OK... the website is looking good and it is well-maintained. Good for you. You're ahead of most.

Google, Bing and Yahoo are the major search engines. At the time of this writing... Google controls about 65% of the search market. Bing is a distant second. Yahoo is next. Bing actually powers most of Yahoo's results. Meaning... Yahoo and Bing struck a ten-year deal in 2009 for Yahoo to license Bing's technology. Yahoo does layer their own "style" on their search results but the fact is Yahoo does not develop much search technology anymore. Yahoo lost to Google a long time ago. In 2015 Yahoo struck another deal with Google to layer Google's technology on top of their search engine.

For a small businesses with a local footprint you must ask yourself three questions to determine how intense your "SEO" should be...

3 questions...

1. "What are we selling?"
2. "Where are we selling it?"

3. "Who else is selling it?"

Fact is... if there are not that many competitors selling what you're selling in your defined geography you really do not need "SEO." A well-built site will do the trick in a smaller market.

If you're business is in a competitive market - chances are you might need some SEO work. Start by getting a detailed ranking report of where you stand. http://www.cyberspacetoyourplace.com/seo-audit/

SEO is unique to your business and ever-evolving. Adjustments must be made. The basics are a well-built site and a clear business identity including proper citations and a strong local presence.

Buyer Beware! No "SEO company" should quote you prices for "SEO" until they first see exactly where you stand for the specific keywords you want to be found for!

Chapter 4:

The Simple Secrets to an Awesome Online Reputation Marketing

Complaints, Compliments... you have heard both. If you have been around long enough you remember the days of Zagat and the Better Business Bureau. Both still exist. But now... reviews and word of mouth move quickly on social media and review sites like Yelp and Google Local. I think it all started with Amazon product reviews. Everyone thought Amazon founder, Jeff Bezos, was crazy for allowing customers to say whatever they wanted about any product. Bezos obviously knew what he was doing.

Yahoo local and Yelp were in the "review" game before Google. There are now countless places where someone can talk (good or bad) about your business.

The main places are...

Facebook: Even though Facebook is really not a "review site" they keep making strides to push reviews. Plus, Facebook is social so it is perfect for positive (or negative) word of mouth. Folks can simply use their newsfeed to say what they want about you. They could "tag" your business as they talk about it. They could go to your business Facebook page and leave a star rating. So... Facebook is a review site and you can guarantee it plays into your online reputation. And... Facebook as a review platform for local businesses will keep evolving. At the end of 2015 Facebook quietly rolled out a local search engine based totally on reviews and ratings.

Google: Google has its "local component." Known right now as "Google My Business." I say "right now" because Google has changed this product so much in the past few years it is hard to keep up. How it works is your business data gets aggregated and a "Google Page" is created. This usually happens for most businesses if they want it to happen or not. Meaning – it's there even if you didn't ask for it. You can "claim" your business listing. From there you can add photos and content to it. Once claimed you can reply to any reviews and you can also respond to any negative reviews. Verifying your Google listings is local internet marketing kindergarten.

Yelp: Yelp is ONLY a local business review site/app. It is not a search engine, even though "Yelpers" do use Yelp to search for things. I like Yelp, but mainly for restaurants. When I am out of town I will often skip Google and go right to my Yelp app. I read reviews. I consider a high volume of reviews as a sign... "this place is busy!" Then, I will click over to the website and online menu to get a feel. I am always turned off if the website and online menu for the place is crappy, bad on a mobile device or simply does not exist. My wife is even more critical as she really, really wants to see an exact menu!

Interesting thing about Yelp. Yelp's artificial intelligence actually knows when a review is "fake." They know (most of the time) when a good review has been rigged or a bad review is some A-hole with a chip on his shoulder. They protect their reviews because it is the main driver of their business. Without solid reviews Yelp has no business.

Yahoo and Bing: Interesting about Yahoo. They were one of the first players in the "local online market." Over the years as their business went in several directions they got away from "Yahoo Local." Plus, they lost eyeballs to Google and Yelp. Now... as mentioned before... they are pulling Bing's search technology and also brining in Yelp reviews. But, strangely enough, at the time of this writing, their Yahoo Local review engine still exists.

Bing is well... Bing. Microsoft's struggling but scrappy search engine meant to take on Google. And of course they offer a local "Bing for Business" listing or whatever it is. Just see the Google paragraph. Understand you most-likely will not see many reviews on your Bing page. PS – they also pull in Yelp data.

OK... Those are the big dogs and if all four are big dogs... Google and Yelp are Great Danes and Yahoo and Bing are like Boxers (one more dog metaphor coming)... which means the rest are like... dachshunds. (Those are the tiny hotdog looking things. My dog, Lucky, thinks they are cats.) But... and there is always a but...

The rest of the local databases are small potatoes compared to the big four. But they are still relevant. Plus, some are "stand-outs" in the niches they serve. Think Trip Advisor or Houzz. When we do a local search marketing campaign we maximize almost 93 of these directories to create solid "back links" and citations. This creates a clear business identity.

Now you can focus on getting more reviews and building a solid business reputation online because you now have the basics.

To start...

You will want to focus your attention on Yelp and Google. Of course, Facebook makes sense too and don't forget the "niche" review platforms.

But Yelp and Google is where your reviews and online reputation (Good or Bad) will have the most impact. So why not let them help you? Reviews do matter and you can tip the scales in your favor with a solid online reputation.

Quick story. We had to go to Hollywood, Florida for one of my daughters to compete in a dance competition. We were hungry when we landed! As we waited for our bags I searched on Yelp for a healthy place to eat. I found this place with smoothies/wraps /yada yada. So, we told the cab driver to take us there. (Uber was banned from the airport – so to run up the fair the cab driver pretended not to know where the place was... JERK!). When we got there we noticed a little shrine to Yelp. It was all about how their Yelp reviews created some crazy increase in business. That's why we ended up there –go figure!

No one will do your push-ups for you when it comes to online reviews. You have to ask your clients and customers to help you. Some will do it on their own. Unfortunately... our world finds it easier to complain rather compliment. You have to encourage but not bribe for good feedback.

As review sites have become more relevant and prolific – Google has given local businesses with a stronger review presence more clout in local rankings. As always, no one really knows or can claim to know Google's formula for ranking. You can only add up all factors and look for the variables.

Reviews are something no local business can ignore.

I find businesses fit into one of three categories when it comes to reviews...

1. On their game: Businesses that are on their game get reviews via two methods. By default. Example: I'm from Philly, originally. You may have heard of Pat's

Steaks? I have talked to the owners on a couple of occasions. When I had a martial arts school in Philly, the owner's granddaughter was a student for a while with us. One thing I know is these guys really do not do a bunch of marketing because they don't have to. And I know they couldn't care less about reviews and online reputation.

Pat's Steaks is just one of the unique businesses where you can throw all of these ideas and marketing concepts out the window. Pat's has not even claimed their Google or Yelp listings. They have a 3.5 out of 5 star rating and they ain't losin' sleep over it. Pat's has 168,000 check-ins on Facebook and they do not do anything with their Facebook page!

The point is... some businesses get reviews by simple volume. If they are busy enough – just the numbers game alone causes them to get reviews. If the food is awesome and the service top-notch, by default a good restaurant can easily get a 4.0 or 5.0 rating. In the case of Pat's Steaks and their 3.5 overall rating it's mainly due to the basic unfriendliness of their staff. (I am not complaining – I like it!) Have you ever been there? It's fun. Depending on the time of the day you go... you stand in a long line and wait your turn. When you get up to the window you are expected to know "how to order a Philly steak." You place your order, the woman or man takes you money as they look through you and into the street. They slide your steak to you and shout... "Next!" Some customers who don't like that customer service model will surely leave a bad review... but again... Pat's doesn't care! Even though Pat's does nothing to get reviews they are still "on their game" because of how busy they are.

The next type of "on their game" business does not have the volume of a Pat's Steaks and they can be in any type of business. These businesses have adapted what I call the C.A.S. method for a powerful online reputation. The "C" stands for Culture. They recognize we are in a culture that values reviews. So they ingrain this culture into their team and employees. The "C" in the formula also means there is a high level of awareness around customer and client reviews.

The "A" in the formula stands for "Ask." If you don't ask you will not get. It's that simple. Asking can never take the form of bribes. Ever! You just have to ask at the right time. You must work this asking into your communication. It can be done during check-up calls or it can be done when the job, the meal is complete or the minor goal is achieved. Asking also gets done as soon as someone gives you a compliment. When you get a compliment it is time to pounce!

The "S" in the formula ties it all together. It stands for System. There is no magic in the system except for working the first two letters and doing it all the time. The system NEVER stops. Ever!

The challenge with being on your game and working the system is usually centered around customers, clients and members having to sign up for an account with Yelp or Google to leave you a review. This is a good thing! Because it helps protect the reviews. Facebook is the same way with their reviews. No fake people hiding behind the internet can leave a review (most of the time).

There are two ways to approach this...
One -- Live with it and realize it will always be a numbers game because not everyone will go through the trouble of leaving the review on Google or Yelp, etc. Two - You can beat it. The software we sell helps you gather reviews at one central point. It also stores all of your reviews in one area. Then, the "Reputation Marketing Ninja" automates the process and encourages happy clients, customers and members to make any 4.0 or 5.0 reviews also available on Yelp, Google and Facebook, etc. It is a powerful resource.

Check out:
http://www.reputationdomination.ninja/help.html

2. Off Their Game: I doubt anyone "off their game" when it comes to reviews are even reading this. But, here goes. It's simple. They are off their game because they have a low online rating. There are too many bad reviews or just too few reviews period and most are bad. To even get an average rating Google requires a minimum amount of reviews. I think the

number of reviews Google uses is five. Picture a business having five reviews and most being three or less stars? Guess what... Poor Rating.

Businesses are off their game because they are usually confused on how to fix a negative online reputation. They actually believe the reviews can be removed. Nope! And obviously, something else is off because why else would they have such a poor rating?

3. Almost Non-Existent: Believe it or not fifty percent of small businesses out there do not have a website of their own or control their own web presence. Everything out there on the web to represent them is a bunch aggregated data from various sources. Their Google Page, Yelp Page, etc. is not owner-verified. These businesses are obscure online.

It some cases this is perfectly fine. Because the business is not effected at all by the web. In short... the web and any sort of online marketing really don't apply. The truth is – many business think they are in this category, but they are often mistaken. I often joke when speaking to audiences how Warren Buffet's business is not affected by his old and out-dated website.

But sadly... most businesses that have crappy websites or no online footprint at all are not Buffet. And they are simply being apathetic and ignorant or maybe arrogant. I doubt there is any help for someone with the qualities of apathy, ignorance and arrogance shining through.

For some additional information about review strategies visit...

http://www.reputationdomination.ninja/help.html

And be sure you check our Google Review page...

https://plus.google.com/+Cyberspacetoyourplacedotcom/about?hl=en

Chapter 5:

The "Push-Button" Secret Hiding in Plain Sight

Email Marketing:

So 1999? It seems like email marketing has been around since forever. The good news... Email Marketing is more relevant an effective now than it has ever been. Sure... there's more competition in the inbox, but if you can learn how to stand out like a violin in marching band – you will get results.

A few basics.

Email marketing is NOT, BCC'ing all of your contacts with your message.

Email marketing is NOT collecting business cards at a networking event and then blasting emails out to all of those people. You will only annoy them!

Finally... Good email marketing is NOT spam! The "Can Spam Act" of 2004 classifies Spam as an unsolicited commercial email. It's when you email someone about business and there has been no previous touch-point. It is worse and becomes true spam when this is done in bulk.

In the early days of the internet – most companies would post email addresses on websites – with the hope that prospects would see those email addresses and contact them. Sure... it worked, but it also enabled spammers free access to email addresses. These spammers would use software to harvest these addresses and send bulk messages. Way back when there was not a lot of competition for attention in the in-box, before spam filters were born – you can bet these early spammers made tons of cash. Sure, they pissed off a ton of people in the process too. Once this (spam) became common the game was on and then quickly over with much-needed Government intervention and spam filters.

Again... Spam is unsolicited with no previous contact. I gave you this history lesson so you can get the right perspective on email marketing and spam.

What Spam is NOT... Spam is not an email marketing piece or an email newsletter sent to folks who have given you permission or implied permission to contact them via email. Implied permission can be anything from a verbal yes to a head nod.

It's about pre-framing. Pre-framing is about setting the frame properly with the goal of controlling perceptions. If you interact with someone and ask them if it is OK for you to add them to your email newsletter list and they say... "sure thing," you now have permission. To take it a step further pre-framing can also be done during the first email correspondence. Which leads to the concept of...

Double Opt-In. A double opt in is when the prospect/email recipient clicks on a link that confirms they want to receive your email pieces. This is actually both technical and important in the grand scheme of things. Email marketing software (and there tons of options here) is what is used to send bulk email. Email Marketing software companies need to protect the integrity of their sending mail servers. A double opt-in usually equals a recipient that will not reach for the spam complaint button.

The practice of double opt-in and pre-framing properly helps keep your email marketing list as clean as possible. Of course, you can have all of the safeguards in place and still offend some very fragile wallflowers. That's why, what's next is most important...

Doing the Email Marketing...

Studies show email marketing has a return of $40 earned for every $1 spent. Meaning... the time you spend doing email marketing - The time you spend crafting the message and the cost of your email marketing software... Add all of these add up and calculate your return. Email marketing works.

I am often asked... "How often should I send out emails to

my list of prospects, customers and clients?" The answer really does depend on your business. Some can get away with the barebones minimum and do once per month. Others must do once a week. And there are some businesses that do email marketing daily.

My rule... Do what works for you but don't be shy about it. When you have information to share along with a relevant offer – you should email! If you're an expert at what you do – you should be emailing your folks. And, it is perfectly OK to offer deals and specials. You just have to have fun, inform your list and be smart about it.

Building an Email List...

NO... You will not go out and purchase a list. Lists must be built over time with the right marketing and compelling reasons for someone to want to be on your list in the first place. You can build your list using multiple angles...

Website Offers
- Landing Page Offers
- Networking
- Shows
- Offline Marketing
- SEO
- Social Media
- Offers inside of your mobile app
- In person during customer/client/prospect

Chapter 5

interactions

The take-away is...

In all of your interactions about your business your mission is two-fold. One - to gain clients and customers. Two, to add folks to your email list so you can to keep in touch with them.

Last Tip...

Don't be uptight and "stuffy" about email marketing. Have fun and be conversational.

Chapter 6:

Are You Nuts Not to Have One of These?

Mobile Apps

If you are still not sure what a mobile app is VS a mobile-friendly or responsive website you are a tad behind the times. An app is downloadable in the Apple App Store or the Google Play store. Yes... Amazon, Windows Store (or whatever it's called) – these are all other places where you can also download apps. But Windows and Amazon are nothing compared with the Play Store and the App Store.

The one thing you have to understand about mobile apps. They are mainly for customer/client/member engagement and retention. Sure... prospects can download your app too, but the safest play and ROI calculation is to assume your app is there to re-engage the folks you already have a relationship with. At the time of the first writing of this book, the chatter is about how Google will begin "indexing" mobile apps in their search results.

Native...

It is a powerful point of contact when your customer/client or prospect decides to download your mobile app. They are inviting you into their world via that valuable piece of real estate... known as the screen on their device. (Mainly their smartphone).

Apps for Small Business Marketing...

When I talk to people about the kind of apps we build or when I am training new salespeople to represent our company I often have to explain how the types of apps we build are for small business marketing.

When pop-culture thinks of mobile apps they think of Instagram, Uber and the many other billion dollar apps out there. There is a big difference between building a mobile app to conquer the world or kill the taxi industry (Uber) VS building an app to market your business.

An app for your small business marketing simply becomes an additional marketing channel. You have to hustle to let your prospects, customers and clients know about your app... then... you use the app to engage with them and stay connected.

Your mobile app becomes a convenient place for your audience to absorb more content from your business. Images, videos, upcoming events, news, notices, ordering, sharing and interaction.

The Crazy Thing About Mobile Apps...
I wrote the first draft of this short book at the end of 2015.

These are not exact stats... but I think something like 70+% of Americans have smartphones and only 5% of small businesses have embraced the power of a mobile app to connect with then on their devices. Do you see the shortfall here? Something needs to change soon!

You can get ahead of the curve with a mobile app. I am including a link to a video presentation on our website about mobile apps and how to use them. And if you like to read, (obviously you do!) below is the transcript of that same video.
http://www.cyberspacetoyourplace.com/services/mobile-apps/

Mobile Apps for Small Businesses

I decided to add this section to the book. It's a transcript of recorded webinar I did on the topic of key mobile app features and functions you will want to employ.

When we talk about mobile apps for small business, we really talk about using the mobile app as a marketing tool, and the reality that mobile app for a small company is actually a marketing channel. We're not talking about creating a mobile app that becomes, you know, a business unto itself and gets purchased for several million dollars; we're talking about engaging with your customers, your clients, your prospects, on the screen and screens that they consume the most content. We're talking about smartphones, and we're talking about tablets.

Now, for illustrative purposes— and I'll remind you a couple of times during this recording— we are using screenshots from smartphones, you know, for example an iPhone or say a Samsung Galaxy, but everything we are talking about here also applies to a tablet, and you'll also notice where some features that we are going to discuss will be better suited for a tablet as well. But, we're talking smartphones here. At the time of this transcript, we are at close to 80%, in the U.S., of consumers have smartphones, and out of that, those are really the kind of customers and clients that you really want for your business. So anyway, let's go ahead and get started.

Alright, then I'm going to pop over here, go to my Powerpoint, and we're just going to go ahead and start the slideshow. So, bear with me, nothing fancy. I wanted to really just keep this simple for you; I was more concerned with getting this recorded webinar finished, rather than putting any bells and whistles together for you.

We're going to explore the power of mobile apps for your business, and as a company, we really focus on a few different industries. We try not to be all things to all people. So, you're going to see a lot of examples from the fitness industry, you know fitness studios, as an example, martial arts, as an example, and also food and plumbing. Alright now, what we just narrowed down were service companies— how we can use apps in service business, we're going out and performing services, and also people are coming to us in the case of fitness or food.

We're going to highlight several different examples from different industries, and I find that the reason why you want to use examples from different industries— why I'm not just creating a webinar for you, a video for you that is all about food, which I could, one that's all about how to use it for a fitness studio, one that is all about how to use it for say a service company or a plumbing company— is because what we find, and this truth has been told over and over, I mean it's validated over and over again, is that when you look at things from various industries, you get better ideas. Meaning, when you're not just myopically focused on your particular line of work, your particular business, your industry, you can see how other folks in almost completely different fields, all small businesses, are using the marketing, using the technology, and then you can sort of massage an idea. And that is where the best innovation actually is going to come, is when you look outside. Of course, pay attention to what is going on in your industry and all of the innovations; I mean, there's a lot there to keep up with, but also look outside of your industry. So just make sure you get over the fact that we're looking at multiple, multiple industries here.

Before we get to mobile apps, we're going to cover the mobile bases, and one of the main mobile bases is that, twofold. One is your website, your mobile website, your responsive website— remember that word, responsive website— that is where most of your new prospects, new customers, are typically going to find— a high percentage of your newer folks, your newer leads, your newer guests, your newer customers, your newer clients— they're going to find you through your main website. Or, they're going to be searching on their mobile device, and they're going to come across what we call, hopefully, your responsive website. All websites now need to be built responsive. That means that it's one website, and it conforms to every screen. Now, the thing to keep in mind is— this is a technical term— we don't just want to smush around the content. We really want to be careful about how we program a responsive website. So, this first slide is just to show you, and remind you, that your website needs to be a multi-screen engagement tool. Same exact URL, all the same content written for all screens, but adjusts to every screen. So, just keep that in mind. Those are the mobile basics.

Alright, so why a mobile app?

I'm going to really tell you a lot of things that you probably already are suspecting. And that's the fact that, I want to say that 90 percent of your best customers, your best prospects, your best guests, your best clients, are using smartphones. They're either using Android smartphones or they're using iOS, like an iPhone, or they're using Android tablets, which there is many, many manufacturers of hardware that make Android tablets, or they're using an iOS tablet, obviously one of the most popular tablets. And what just recently got dethroned is the iPad, although there is still a ton of iPads out there, where we are at now is Android tablets because there are just so many more manufacturers of Android tablets have made the iPad second fiddle, if you will, even though the iPad was first in the space. Myself, personally, just to reveal about my hardware habits, I have a Windows 10 Dell laptop that I'm recording this on. I have a Galaxy S6 at the time of this recording, and I also have an iPad 2 tablet. You know, all three work for me, and I do that just to purposely bounce around. But anyway, why a mobile app is because this is where the eyeballs are, and you can fact-check all of this. The consumption of content on mobile devices is huge and growing. I know that's a pretty generic or vague number, huge and growing, but it is.

Most content is being consumed on smartphones these days, and the good news is it is not eclipsing say, the desktop or the laptop just yet, it's just adding to it. So what we really are doing is we are competing for attention. Sure, there's competition down the street; there's competition in your neighborhood; there's competition in your area for your similar service or your business, but you're also competing for the attention. So, it's a channel, the mobile app is a channel for you to get attention from your prospects, your customers, and anyone who is going to be referred to you. So that's why you want a mobile app because this is where we are, and you have a good change to jump ahead of your competition and use a mobile app as a channel to engage your best prospects, your best customers, your best referrals, your best clients. Alright, so that's why a mobile app—because this where we are, and where we're going, and where we're going to be for quite a while.

We are just going to go through some different concepts of a mobile app, and how this all works in terms of feature equals benefits. Now, one of the things I really enjoy about mobile apps is the fact that referrals are made easy. Meaning, let's imagine if I am in the need for, say, a plumbing service, and I happen to express that to my neighbor, or something—maybe my hot water tank just is starting to go, or I know I need to get some filters cleaned, or I need some service because I haven't heard from the other guy that I dealt with—whatever the case may be, and I happen to ask somebody, "Hey Bill. Do you know any good plumbers?" And he says, "Well yeah, I know, I know Paul the Plumber." And I say, "Oh, okay great. Do you have his number?" And he says, "Well you know what, why don't I go ahead an share his app with you." And he has the app, the plumbing company app, on his smartphone, and he just taps the share button, and when he taps the share button, he chooses to send it via SMS, and now I have all of the contact information, everything I need to really just engage with that company right there on my phone. So, it's almost like your business can go— the term is viral, and it's really amazing. And you can prompt your customers to do this; you can have some fun sort of reminding clients to refer you via the app. Hopefully it's fun for them as well, but at the very least, you have a default tool for referrals made easy. Same thing, picture your food business, your restaurant; people are sharing it with their friends because they're happy.

One of the things I like, and this doesn't apply to every single business, and it's okay, but one of the things you really need to be doing is embracing video online. Obviously we're doing, using video right now. You really want to embrace video online because it's a huge part of mobile— again, there's that word again, huge— it's a big part of mobile content consumption is watching videos on your tablet. Again, everything here applies to tablets; we're just using the iPhone and the Android images just to make things simple. But, videos are huge, and it's not a big deal. Each business can use videos a little differently. So, you know, if you're in the fitness business, obviously this happens to be a martial arts situation where the gentlemen is kind of talking to a group of kids, kind of giving them what they call in the martial arts world a mat chat. But picture awesome videos from your food place with the new dish that you're doing, and what happens is really simple. And you know, this is not hard; a company like ours, we try to help our clients with this; we can explain it to you; we can do it for you, but here's how it would work. You can take a video with a professional camera, or you can take a video with say, a smartphone, and you can record whatever you want. So, now we have this example.

Let's use the example of recording that awesome new dish that's just came off the grill there, or whatever the case may be, that's steaming, and you can almost smell it through the video because it looks so appetizing, and you're putting that video on your YouTube channel— which is a good idea for marketing anyway, like I said you need to be embracing video no matter what— and now that is also going to sync right to your app, and then you're going to send out a notice that says, "hey, look at today's special," or "look at this awesome dish we just invented," or whatever the case may be. Imagine that, your customers and clients being able to watch a video of you explaining the ingredients or just whatever it is. It's just an amazing way to just stay in contact, and almost just trump the competition. So, videos are awesome, and obviously we'll get you more examples as we go along. So, video inside your app, very powerful.

Another thing I like too is contests, points, social, and these will all boost engagement. So if you look at the image on your screen right, in here what you have is what we call the fan wall. And inside the fan wall, we're able to sort of interact and talk to our customers, and our clients, and our members, and just sort of keep the conversation going, and invite them to engage and participate. You know, the more they're engaging with your business and participating, the more loyal they're becoming. Now if you look at your screen left, we're going to look over at the very— let's just say the very simple example, especially for the food industry— which in this case is "Purchase Five Pizzas, Get the Sixth for free." How this works is it works just like any loyalty card except it's never lost. So, here, our staff has a secret code of whatever the special is, obviously you have to do a little work in making sure the staff knows what it is— it's worth it— and you're giving your folks a loyalty reward. You know, someone is purchasing five pizzas, and you can even put it in a certain date. You can say, "purchase five within a month," or whatever the case may be, "get the sixth for free." You're rewarding that loyalty, and you're also going to boost consumption, and you can use the point system for anything. Obviously the best example is in the food world where you get the sixth, or the tenth, or the eleventh item on the house because you are loyal. Alright, so the loyalty system is awesome.

Okay, so easy communication that gets through. So now, your communication here is your push notice, and this is an example from actually a fitness studio that my wife owns, and you know we're basically sending a notice out that says, "hey, the cardio-kick class starts at five o'clock." Now, this goes right to the stream of the smartphone, right to the notification; it gives a little ding when it comes through, a little notice with a quick bite-size message, and it's okay. They're 120, 130 characters, and that's the reality we live in is the fact that we consume content in bite-size chunks. So now, this notice goes out as a reminder, and this can be anything— it can be a reminder to do something, it can be a special. What I really love about the push notifications is also, now pay attention here, is what we call geo-fencing push notices. If you have a local business, let's just say a local eatery, food, whatever the case may be, you are going to be able to create a geo-fence. That means, in a certain area, as soon as that smartphone crosses that fence, your customer can get a notice of whatever special, and it's called proximity marketing, geo-fence marketing. It's really powerful and pretty amazing. So, the push notifications enable easy communication, and you can send out a hundred of these a month, or you can send out ten-thousands of them. That's the beauty of it. You can send out all kinds of messages here and boost communication that way. So, easy communication that gets through.

Okay, I really love the fact that you're getting your customer, your prospect, your client, to actually consume your content. We love looking at pictures and images online— if you don't believe me, that's why Facebook bought Instagram for a billion dollars. That's why when you go to your Facebook News Feed where you look at things online, it's very visual because we love to look at photos through our smartphones because it is so easy. So, consumption of photos and images via smartphones and tablets is just huge— there's that word again because it's true. All of this is just very big so you can get your folks to consume your own media, and every time they're engaging with you, they are taking a step toward more loyalty with your business, and you're just outdoing your competition. I love the gallery function because you can add some photos, and people can consume them. You have to think outside of the box here. Now, this is an example of a fitness business, right, a lot of fun, a little motivation there, alright, enjoyable thing there. Now let's picture other, just for a second, close your eyes or just picture another phone here, and let's talk about how the plumbing contractor possibly just did a new install, remodel bathroom— people love looking at that stuff, especially women enjoy seeing what the potential is in home remodeling— also picture the food business, the delicious looking dishes that people can get excited about and come in and purchase. So you really have to— just put your thinking cap on for just a second and know that if you have a service company, food establishment, or fitness type business, this is going to apply to you, and obviously we can help you with this.

Alright, I love events, schedules, and reservations. You know, if you're doing some events in your business— if you look far left on your screen, you can see a whole list of events. You know how easy it is not to miss anything or choose which events your customers want to register for and participate in, and they can almost say, "hey, I wonder what we can do next week," and they can just pop in, look at your events. You can also send notices about upcoming events and lead them right to the event area. So there's just a lot of potential here in listing out your events so people know what's coming up, that you take the guesswork out of it, and they can plan it; it's pretty amazing. If you look screen middle, you see reservations and obviously screen right you see another set of reservations. So, you have reservations. If you're a business that needs to take reservations, then you can simply do it right through your app. Now, we're using the food example, but also reservations can translate to appointments as well. If you have a business that relies on people making, scheduling appointments, it can all be done efficiently right through the app. Pretty amazing.

Deals. Everyone loves a good deal, so you can almost have a whole set of coupons inside your app to reward that loyalty. Anything you can do to let people know they're getting a good deal and again, reward their loyalty and consumption, is going to be very powerful. You can have a whole list— I mean in this case, this gentleman has a whole list of things that are going to be done for the whole week, and each one I can click on to see what the deal is. So, the beat the clock deal, I can tap that with my thumb then it can show me what it is. The Two for Tuesday deal, I can click that. The Wacky Wednesday deal, I can click that, so this is pretty amazing. And again, deals— your best customers and clients do deserve some reward, and you want to use the app to increase, you know repeat business and consumption. If you were to think about the main reason for an app, it's again to engage your customers and clients; it's branding, you know you're on the device— as my plumber company clients say, it's the fridge magnet, the new fridge magnet; there's also communication, and there's reward, and boosting referrals. So boosting referrals, boosting engagement, getting more repeat business. Those three things: boost engagement, boost referrals, get more repeat business. That's really going to be the key to your mobile app. That's why you need one.

Okay, online ordering. This totally applies just to the food world, alright, but you can also have your online ordering here where you may want to take some orders in advance for your food business. This is totally just a food example here, but, so you can see, you can just add the cart, checkout, restaurant gets the order, and you have it ready for your customer when they show up, so that's really cool. So it's pretty much mobile ordering, which is pretty amazing all right through the app, convenient, very simply— not for everyone. We have some clients that just want their customer to just pick up the phone, which I can respect as well. So, it's not for everyone, but it's a good feature.

You can capture leads through your app as well and get them on your newsletter, so that's something you want to keep in mind is that you can offer them the chance to sign up for a newsletter, and now they can start getting emails from you as well. You want to embrace all forms of technology, so you can definitely capture leads. In this case— because you don't really know the names of people that download your app, but if you give them a way to also engage with you, like in this case for a fitness studio. Three pairs of gloves for nineteen bucks, I'm sorry— three classes and a pair of gloves for nineteen dollars, name, last name, email, and of course, you can't see it, but you can get the mobile phone as well. Now you actually have a real, live customer or a real, live lead. So, they went from mobile app download who you have no way to really tell who they are to actually capturing a lead, a real person who you can call and actually do business with. So capturing leads is very powerful.

So, that's it. Those are the core. I told you I wanted to keep it simple. Again, I'll reinforce the main drivers for why you want to have a mobile app. One is to boost engagement, branding, live there on the device that your customers check 50-plus or 100-plus times a day, and then you also want to drive referrals through share function. You want to drive consumption, alright, which boosts engagement, and you want to drive repeat business. So the time really is now, make sure you reach out to us at CyberSpacetoYourPlace.com or MyOnlineMarketingConnection.com, and let's talk about how to get your mobile app. In fact, let's put a demo together for you. Let's put one together for you that's totally your business, and you can actually see how it would look.

Chapter 7:

KEEP It Fresh

Websites are meant to be dynamic. It is so sad to see so many websites out there representing small businesses that have not been updated in years. Static is the word I am looking for.

It doesn't have to be this way! Websites are easy to update these days. WordPress powers almost 20% of the entire web. It is the platform we build most sites on. We always make sure each site has a solid blog, news area and recent projects or upcoming events area.

Be an expert in your business. Post valuable information to your blog. Inform your market. Keep them in the know.

News about your business and industry... You can use your website as a tool to post news and developments about your business.

Events and Recent Projects... If you have a business that promotes events your website is a simple way to spread the word. If you have the type of business that works on visual projects... think home remodeling... etc... Your website can be a place to showcase recent work and show your market things are happening with your business.

Why Bother?

Simple... Keeping your website updated shows your prospect your business has a pulse. As they are checking you out they get a good vibe because they see things are happening. There are studies that show consumers trust a business with an updated website over one with an outdated and stale website.

Search Engines...

Google and Bing love fresh content. Google more than Bing. Every time you post a blog Google and Bing have a reason to come back and index the pages in search.
When is a good time? Any time really... Just be consistent.

Chapter 8:

The Linchpin of Social Media Marketing (And Maybe ALL Marketing)

Facebook Advertising:

I don't want to spoil your fantasy in case you foolishly thought Facebook was free. Facebook is NOT FREE. Not if you actually want to get some results. Facebook is meant for its users. The users are the product. The data Facebook collects on you and me has a high value to advertisers that know what they are doing. The balance that Facebook has to achieve (and does a great job achieving) is the fact that users would rather not see any ads. But, users know, for the most part, Facebook has to pay its bills. That's why Facebook Ads can be so powerful.

The targeting is based on the user's likes and profile. Facebook is what we call an "interruption marketing media." That just means unlike Google, a Facebook user does not really go to Facebook seeking anything out. The user goes to Facebook to be a voyeur and a narcissist all under one roof. And that is the only reason they go back day after day, hour after hour.

Now for your big let-down moment...

In 2012 I wrote an entire book on Facebook Ads strategy. The problem is this... Facebook has changed so many things over the years and continues to change. That's why in this book I can only tell you one thing...

If you and your business are serious about marketing.... Facebook Ads is a MUST. You either, go in and figure it out or you hire an agency and a consultant to help you. We do help several clients with Facebook Advertising campaigns and strategy.
As to not totally let you down here's a list of top Facebook Ad Strategies...

Be consistent with your content.

Promote "warm and fuzzy/engaging content" just as much as you promote deals and special offers.

Video is big. Facebook is growing more and more every day. Use video to your advantage. Don't be shy about it.

Landing pages and lead generation ads hold the key to ROI from Facebook Marketing. Driving ads to landing pages with a specific call to action can help you keep your lead funnel filled, your email list growing and your business top of mind.

Use Re-Marketing. Re-Marketing is powerful. We can do this two ways. One, place code on your website to "pixel" web visitors so you can then remarket to them on Facebook.

Upload your email list to Facebook and Facebook can cross-reference those emails with matches for Facebook users. You can stay in front of the Facebook users who already know you a little bit.

Experience matters...

Facebook is constantly changing and evolving their ads platform but I have noticed the principles have stayed the same since 2010. Experience helps you navigate these changes. Most changes are built on and are improvements on the current product. To publish anything too deep in a book about Facebook Ads is foolish so you won't catch me doing it anymore. You either gain the wisdom and the experience or you work with someone who does.

Learn more about how we work with clients and help them with Facebook Ads here...

http://www.cyberspacetoyourplace.com/services-2/facebook-marketing/

Chapter 9:

What to Say

Social Media Content

Ahh... the question... "Should we outsource social media content?"

Simple answer... Not really.

The fact is the best social media content comes from within your small business. It comes from your ability to develop some sort of framework around your social media marketing.

It starts with choosing the best social platform. The best platform is the one your prospects, customers, clients and members are on. At the time of this writing... Facebook is the juggernaut we all share. Facebook is the one place where most of our prospects are. Facebook is the one place where mountains of data has been collected on your target market.

But sure...

An Instagram strategy will definitely reach a younger and engaged audience.

Snapchat may help you story-tell to a young social media user loyal to Snapchat.

Twitter... well... no one knows. Seriously... I have always said Twitter was best for news outlets and celebs.

At one point we thought Tumblr would be the way to reach urban folks. Maybe it still is... but since Yahoo bought it... who knows??

Pinterest has always been mostly women. And the studies show it can really drive some online sales. Maybe you can use it?

LinkedIn... for B2B peeps and sales pros. LinkedIn has many layers to what you can do there and you'll get more traction if you pay for their added services. Is their paid plan worth it? You be the judge.

I know I forgot... Google+ and YouTube.

I also did not mention the new popular live-streaming mobile apps... Periscope and Meerkat. These apps allow you to live broadcast to your followers. Side-note: At the time of this writing Facebook is moving down the path of enabling live broadcasting for brands and businesses.

Here's the problem with all these platforms...

The old joke...

"You don't want to try to sell me anything as I can't afford to pay... ATTENTION!"
Attention is one of the most valuable things next to time. Attention is time.

The attention problem has two elements for us small business owners.

Chapter 10

The Smart Money Uses
Landing Pages

Promotional Pages (landing pages) to Match All Marketing is what we're going to talk about next.

Do you want to be savvy with all of this online marketing stuff?

Then... become a landing page monster! I joke that I have tons of landing pages - I just need the $500,000 ad budget to promote them.

Seriously... You don't need that much in your ad budget to promote landing pages. A few dollars per day is just fine. Landing pages are what savvy marketers use to clock big ROI from ad dollars.

Think of a landing page as a simple web page focused on one thing...

Driving the visitor to a specific "call to action" and influencing the result you want. Nothing else. Nothing else matters.

Most of your online ad money should point to landing pages to match the specific offer in the ad. Google Ads, Facebook Ads ... everything.

What you need for a landing page...

Short and Pithy AdCopy.
A Strong Call to Action.
A Compelling Offer.

A Way to Capture the Lead and Move them to the Next Step.

A Marketing Funnel.

Easiest example of a landing page...

Check this one out. It's one of my many landing pages. And this one simply drives the visitors to request a quote to redesign their business website. It is focused on problems with out-dated websites. The landing page agitates the problem a little and then offers a solution.

http://www.cyberspacetoyourplace.com/problems/

Chapter 11:

All This "Marketing Stuff" Doesn't Matter Much if You Can't Sell

Sales ...

Sales is the life-blood of your business. If you're not selling at a high level... it's a problem.

Here's my take on (not all) sales training and sales books. Who has time to write sales books (I'm guilty of writing one. I wrote it after I transitioned out of one business into another and had some downtime) if... they are busy selling stuff? Heck, even if you're busy selling the sales training and the sales manuals and book... you still have to be too busy to update things, right? The first sales manual I wrote was written to train people who worked for me.

That's why if I ever do sales training I will NEVER read from a manual or use a manual. I'll just show up and help the sales manager tell his guys and girls what he's been trying to tell them all along.

"Do something, sell something, work smart and work hard, but do both!"

Working Smart in Sales is simple...

It comes down to knowing how not to kill a deal. Working smart in sales comes from understanding the sharp axe concept. You can take whacks at the tree for hours with a dull axe. Or you can make it sharp, take less whacks at the tree and cut the tree down in less time.

No fluff. Your prospects really don't have time for fluff. I get it. Some higher end sales are based on playing golf and going out to dinner with prospects and customers/clients. But ya know what... that's relationship building - not sales. If you get to the point of getting someone to dinner, then I bet you have already closed something. I mean, who wants to eat dinner with people they don't like? What's up with that? People only buy from people they like.

Sales is about smart work and hard work. And never let anyone fool you. Sales is still a numbers game. Sure, it's not just about quantity, it's about quality too. But if you could do quality in large quantities, that's good right? Hard work is your volume and the amount of sales interactions you have on a daily basis. Quality is about what you bring to each interaction.

Doesn't matter the business you're in.

Low ticket sales or high ticket sales with a long sales cycle. Whatever. Sales is sales. Hustle is hustle. Remember Dave

Thomas? The Wendy's founder. He was famous amongst his top executives and operations people for constantly "grilling" (pardon the pun) them on what they were doing to stimulate sales. We're talking bacon cheeseburgers here people!

Phycology, Persuasion and a Touch of Psychopath.

Those are the three P's needed to be awesome at selling.

Never forget you're dealing with the human brain when selling. You are mainly dealing with people's innate fears of losing something or taking a risk. That's why trust is the biggest hurdle in sales. You are dealing with people's weak decision-making muscles. Most people would rather not go through the exertion of making a decision.
Making something out of nothing.

The real sales opportunity is not in selling by default. Yes... of course... Apple makes kick-ass products (I guess) – but it was Steve Jobs who first sold the masses on why we had to have Apple products. Now Apple has to keep that going with their great stuff and their PR engine.

But guess what... making something out of nothing would be taking me...   the stubborn Windows user and Samsung/Android/Google fanboy and converting me to a Mac and an Iphone. For me - no amount of product launch magic will do it. You'd have to sell me, knee to knee and belly to belly. That's making something out of nothing.

The best salespeople make something out of nothing by finding problems to solve and showing suspects and prospects solutions and opportunities. That's the persuasion side. The psycho side comes in the follow up tenacity and ability that's needed to win the game.

That's all for now about sales.

Chapter 12:

Never Be Done

Conclusion:

Well... that's it. Short and simple, right? The truth is this book could have been 200 to 500 pages. It could be an exact step by step guide to marketing. The problem with that is ... one... you wouldn't follow it step by step because you're a stubborn-ass business owner. And two... that would be too long so you wouldn't read it anyway.

I hope you now have some additional perspective. That's exactly what the Consigliere is supposed to give you...Perspective.

What did I leave out?

I left out areas where I am not as qualified to help you. Two in particular. Google Adwords and Networking. I talked about Facebook Ads but not Google Ads. Google is the other place where your ad dollars (invested right) could give you a nice return. Networking consists of deep relationship building with strategic partners and attending the right events to grow your business. Don't overlook Networking. Make time to do it right.

You have to fill in the blanks. You have to deploy the tactics. Sure, we can help you. Ultimately, the buck stops with you. You have to take each of these (and more) and then build on them. Do something every day to move your business forward.

Your success will ultimately come from consistent action every day.

Reach out. Let us know if we can help.

All the best of success to your business.

Mike D.

PS: Call me... 888-500-2365 X 20

PPS: Also check out...

http://www.cyberspacetoyourplace.com/

Also check out (for complete marketing help)...

http://www.cyberspacetoyourplace.com/consiglieri/